To Diego & Mario,
   I will always cherish our fun memories together. May God bless you both with wisdom and a good night's rest. ¡Los quiero muchísimo! -Mami ❤️

Duérmete mi niño,

Will These Brothers Ever Go to Sleep?

Niños, bedtime!

Can we play for five more minutes?

Copyright © 2021 by Jacqueline Leal Lopez

All rights reserved. No part of this book may be reproduced or used in any manner without written permission of the copyright owner except for the use of quotations in a book review. For more information, address: jacquelineleallopez@yahoo.com

Print ISBN: 9781736397909
eBook ISBN: 9781736397916

"Bedtime niños! "It's time to go mimis!"
Mami announced.

As Mario started to yawn, he resisted by saying, "I don't want to go to bed. I'm not sleepy!"

"Can we play for a little while longer?" Diego asked.

"Sorry kiddos. It's time to go to la cama."
Mami responded.

Every night before heading to their room, they sneak in some extra play minutes by:

playing with their toys,

beatboxing,

bm-ch
b-b-k
ts-ts
bts-kats

brushing their teeth,

drawing pictures,

laughing at jokes, telling stories,

and reading books.

The boys finally settled down by saying their nightly prayers and climbing into la cama.

"Mami, will you sleep with us?" Mario asked.

Mario did not like sleeping in the dark, nor did he like to sleep solito. If he had to go to bed, having his familia there would help him fall asleep faster. Mami knew this, so she agreed to come stay with them for a while.

"I'm still not sleepy!" Diego announced.

Mario asked, "Mami, will you sing Duérmete mi niño?"

This song has been one of our favorite bedtime canciones.

Smiling, she responded, "Si mijo, now close your eyes and relájate."

"Yay! I love this song!" Diego added.

As she caressed Mario's hair, she continued to sing the song over and over.

Finally, both boys were sound asleep.

"Buenas noches mis hijos. Goodnight my sweet Angelitos. God bless you both." she whispered.

Then she kissed them goodnight.

Glossary

duérmete- go to sleep
mi niño- my child/son
mami- mommy
la cama- the bed
angelitos- little angels
si mijo- yes, my son
buenas noches- goodnight

niños- boys
familia- family
relájate- relax
canciones- songs
mis hijos- my sons
solito- alone
mimis- sleep

About the Author/Illustrator

Jacqueline Leal Lopez

As a mom and an educator, Jacqueline Leal Lopez knows the importance of routines. Bedtime is no different, as many kids usually don't want to go to bed when they're busy having fun. This song version of "Duérmete mi niño" came about when she decided to personalize it for her baby by changing some of the lyrics. It became a favorite bedtime song that helped her kids settle down and eventually fall asleep. With this story, Jacqueline hopes Diego and Mario will always cherish these fun memories, including two of their drawings featured in this book. She also hopes that you'll enjoy a sneak peek into the life of these fun-loving brothers, who most nights found ways to delay bedtime to sneak in some extra play minutes. Thankfully, routine, love, patience, prayer, and music won over the nightly protests.

To conclude, Jacqueline remembers aspiring to become an author/illustrator after participating in the Young Authors Fair in the fourth grade. Since then, she persevered and earned her Master of Arts Degree in Education from Cal State University, Bakersfield. As an educator, she hopes she can inspire her students to achieve their dreams and aspirations.

www.ingramcontent.com/pod-product-compliance
Lightning Source LLC
Chambersburg PA
CBHW041707160426
43209CB00017B/1764